PRAYERS
TO THE
MOON

Also by Kay Leigh Hagan

Internal Affairs: A Journalkeeping Workbook for Self-Intimacy
Fugitive Information: A Series of Feminist Essays

PRAYERS TO THE MOON

Exercises in Self-Reflection

KAY LEIGH HAGAN

HarperSanFrancisco
A Division of HarperCollins*Publishers*

Kay Leigh Hagan offers workshops and lectures nationally.
For a schedule of upcoming appearances, or for information
on sponsoring one in your area, please write c/o
Escapadia Press, P.O. Box 5298, Atlanta GA 30307.

PRAYERS TO THE MOON: *Exercises in Self-Reflection*.
Copyright © 1991 by Kay Leigh Hagan. All rights reserved. Printed in the United
States of America. No part of this book may be used or reproduced in any manner
whatsoever without written permission except in the case of brief quotations
embodied in critical articles and reviews. For information address HarperCollins
Publishers, 10 East 53rd Street, New York, NY 10022.

Text design by Wendy Calmenson   Moon illustrations by Clyde H. Breitwieser

FIRST EDITION

Library of Congress Cataloging-in-Publication Data

Hagan, Kay Leigh.
    Prayers to the moon: exercises in self-reflection / Kay Leigh
Hagan. —1st ed.
        p.   cm.
    Includes bibliographical references.
    ISBN 0–06–250378–2 (alk. paper)
    1. Self-perception—Problems, exercises, etc.   2. Diaries—
Authorship.   I. Title.
BF697.5.S43H35   1991
158'.1—dc20   90–56470
                                                          CIP

93 94 95 RRD 10 9 8 7 6 5 4 3 2

This edition is printed on acid-free paper that meets the American
National Standards Institute Z39.48 Standard.

For Anna

Contents

Introduction: Evoking the
   Essential Self 1
Ways to Use This Book 5
Suggestions for Group Work 9
Key to the Nautilus Route 11

1. Lake of Dreams 12
2. List of Desires 16
3. Sea of Crisis 20
4. Check In 24
5. Sea of Tranquility 28
6. New Moon 32
7. Personal Mail 36
8. Animal Guide 40
9. Scrutiny 44
10. Breath 48
11. Growing Pains 52
12. Back to Nature 56
13. Intuitrip 60
14. Waning Moon 64
15. Role Model 68
16. Webpoints 72
17. Repetition 76
18. Simple Pleasures 80
19. Independent Study 84

20. Full Circle 88
21. The Other You 92
22. Chinese Clue 96
23. Control 100
24. Home Free 104
25. Waxing Moon 108
26. Nesting 112
27. Eclipse 116
28. Ebb and Flow 120
29. Moonlighting 124
30. Sea of Vapors 128
31. Altar Ego 132
32. Full Moon 136
33. Bay of Rainbows 140
34. The Daily Day 144
35. Integrity 148
36. Alone Time 152
37. Sea of Nectar 156
38. Harvest Moon 160

39. Moonstruck 164
40. Discipline 168
41. Marsh of Sleep 172
42. Ocean of Storms 176
43. Weeding 180
44. Shadow Side 184
45. Marsh of Fog 188
46. Stop/Watch 192
47. Old Friends 196
48. Personal Map 200
49. Totem Story 204
50. The Physical Plane 208
51. Initiating Change 212
52. Ring-Pass-Not 216

Further Study 221
Acknowledgments 229

Introduction: Evoking the Essential Self

THE ESSENTIAL SELF IS CALLED BY MANY NAMES. Spirit, psyche, soul, divine spark, inner power, Be-ing, integrity, intuition, common sense, truth, genius—these are just a few of the words we use to name a certain sense of knowing, ineffable yet clear, that resonates with our hearts and transcends our normal understanding. I choose *essential self* because I experience this deeply personal wisdom as one inner self among many who vie for my attention.

Through the practices of self-reflection and journalkeeping, I have discovered aspects of my self that I perceive as internal voices speaking from different parts of my experience: the confused child, the perfectionist, the performer, the poet, and others. I form these selves throughout my life in response to interactions with family, community, and culture. Some of these aspects are helpful, others filled with fear and self-hatred. What I call the essential self is the pulse of knowing that affirms my being like the vital fluids running through a tree, while layers of bark—the constructed selves—continue to form around the trunk.

Although I see this process as natural, inevitable, and uniquely human, I have come to understand that, unlike the protective bark of a tree, my constructed selves are artificial products of habit and conditioning. They often serve to separate me from that deeper transcendent knowing, limiting my respon-siveness and creativity. One definition of essential is "belonging to the very nature of a thing." When I am in touch with my essential self, then, I am aware of my own nature, the spark of life I share with all beings. To evoke the essential self is to call upon that innate wisdom, consciously and with intention. I have named this sacred practice of self-reflection *praying to the moon*.

The moon's influence on our daily lives is undeniable. We see and feel the moon's effect on the tides, the sap of plants, the magnetic charge of the earth, and our own blood. For urban dwellers surrounded by concrete, steel, and utility wires, the cycles of the moon are sometimes the only way to connect with the rhythms of nature. To people all over the world and over many thousands of years, the moon has also symbolized introspection, intuition, and the unconscious. The moon's light and shadow sides are a reminder of the known and unknown within us, its constantly changing face a mirror of our own continuous cycle of change. For all of these reasons, to me the moon is a symbol of the essential self.

I use the term *prayer* with *moon* knowing it may sound absurd. Usually, prayer is understood as an appeal to a deity for comfort, guidance, or intervention, to express gratitude, or to ask forgiveness. Regardless of how prayer is directed, however, it is the act of focusing conscious attention on our deepest desires and expressing them. To pray is to become still, to speak from the heart, and to listen. *Praying to the moon* suggests poetically that we consciously direct attention to our essence, our profound connection with nature, for in doing so we learn to tell the difference between what is essential in us and what is constructed. One way to begin this sacred work is by observing our own minds, where we form both our view of the world and our self-image—and where awareness of our connection with the natural world begins. Here, in the simplicity of our daily choices, we can discover opportunities to live in intimate harmony with nature.

A sequence of fifty-two exercises, *Prayers to the Moon: Exercises in Self-Reflection* continues the experiential journey of *Internal Affairs: A Journalkeeping Workbook for Self-Intimacy.* These exercises—more about seeing than writing, really—are designed to strengthen the ability to self-observe, to notice the difference between the constructed selves and the essential self, and to become aware of our moments of choice. Most people can write naturally from this depth with this attitude—basically a healthy, intelligent, curious, loving relationship with the self—if they keep a journal consistently for many years. However, my experience teaching workshops in journalkeeping tells me that without encouragement few people will commit themselves to this practice of deep reflection. I created *Prayers to the Moon* to stimulate such a practice, for I believe to the extent we are self-aware, we can make conscious choices. In these uncertain times, developing this ability is central to the deep, authentic change we so urgently need in ourselves and society.

May these prayers to the moon bring you insight, power, and courage.

Kay Leigh Hagan
February 28, 1991
Full Moon

Ways to Use This Book

IN TIBETAN BUDDHIST CULTURE, prayer flags "confide spiritual longings to the winds." As the small flags are gradually worn away by the elements, the prayers are believed to disperse throughout the universe. You might think of the exercises in this book as your weekly "prayer flags," reminding you to seek connection with your essence, releasing your self-awareness into the world.

While this workbook is designed especially for writing, these exercises are not simply suggestions for journal entries but are meant to encourage the development of an inner presence I call the "observer participant." This thoughtful observing self takes careful note of daily interactions, bringing a gentle accepting curiosity and attention to each moment. The observer participant attitude might be called "mindfulness" by Buddhists, "being awake" by followers of the Fourth Way, "Spinning" by Mary Daly, or "contemplation" by Christians.

You will find here meditations, field trips, memory probes, and philosophical questions, asking you in different ways to study your daily habits while noticing specific aspects of your thoughts, beliefs, and feelings. To get the most benefit from this work, I suggest that you read an exercise, write your immediate responses, and then remind yourself of the assignment throughout the week. Observe your daily habits, practice directing your attention to the subtleties of your behavior, and listen. After a few days, return to the workbook to record what you notice. Your insights may not seem dramatic at first, but the practice of self-observation is cumulative, and you will soon make connections that will surprise you.

Here's an example: While observing my relationship with money a few years ago, I heard a quiet but panicky inner voice warning, "The wolf is at the door!" Having lived on a shoestring most of my life, I was more than familiar with the feeling of impending financial crisis, but never before had I heard this repeated warning on a conscious level. I was not particularly short of funds at the time, but I began to notice subtle habits that perpetuated the tension of scarcity even in times of plenty. For instance, much to my amazement, I saw that I habitually bought only one roll of toilet paper at a time, my reasoning being that until I was in dire need of something, I should not buy it! The day I bought my first four-pack, I felt a sheepish pride in taking care of my very basic needs as I waved the wolf away from my door.

If you find yourself being critical, realize that this is not a test or pop quiz: There are no wrong answers. You are simply learning to observe your mind at work. If you find that you persist in being judgmental about what you are seeing and writing and that this inhibits your progress, I suggest reviewing the early chapters of *Internal Affairs: A Journalkeeping Workbook for Self-Intimacy* for suggestions to counter your habits of self-criticism.

You may do the exercises in any order you wish. Look at the titles in the table of contents and use your intuition to select one. Open the book at random. Make up lots you can draw. Or follow one of the two sequences I have created with specific themes.

The *Almanac Route* follows the weeks of the calendar year, with one exercise per week; the dates are noted on the lower-left side of the page. To follow the Almanac Route, begin with the exercise for the current calendar week: If you begin on June 15, start with "Home Free," number 24, for the week of June 11–17. On the Almanac Route, the rhythm of your inner work will subtly mirror the natural cycle of the seasons—winter exercises emphasize mystery, drawing in, and the dormant phase of a seed, while spring exercises pull your focus up and out to the bright energy of birth and growth. The Almanac Route directs your attention alternately from the internal plane to the practical challenges of daily living. (Readers in the Southern Hemisphere should add six months to adjust the seasonal correlation. For example, a reader in the Southern Hemisphere beginning on June 15 would start with "The Physical Plane," number 50, for the week of December 10–16.)

The *Nautilus Route* uses the same exercises as the Almanac Route but in a different order. Named after the chambered nautilus seashell with its spiralling pattern, the Nautilus Route moves in a spiral from the outer layers of your constructed selves to the intimate depths of the essential self. The key to this route lists the sequence in which exercises are to be performed and is on page 11. On the Nautilus Route, you will explore how your self-image is constructed from the outside in, moving past layers of impressions and beliefs that often obscure your essence. This path is in some ways more direct than the Almanac Route, so you may choose to move more quickly than one exercise per week. However, I urge you to keep in mind the goal of practicing self-observation and to give yourself time to study your daily routines. Read and consider each exercise, write your immediate responses, and then let yourself mull over the question for a few days, returning to write your afterthoughts. You are not simply writing in a workbook; you are creating a new mental perspective from which to view your internal process.

Regardless of where you live, the moon can be a constant connection point to the elemental community of nature, and so I have made the moon a strong presence in the workbook itself. Many of the exercises are named after actual lunar sites and characteristics. On the upper-right page corners are a series of images following the moon's cycle of waxing and waning. While these images cannot correlate to the current phase of the moon, they are meant to remind you to follow the moon's cycle, noticing how each phase affects your moods, the plants, and other aspects of your environment. There are many lunar calendars available that chart the moon's phases, so you can follow them daily. In this book, the lower margins contain facts and lore about the moon to broaden your knowledge about our nearest celestial neighbor, and screened in the background of each page is the actual terrain of the moon, allowing you to write your prayers across the moon's surface as you connect with your essential self.

The section called "Further Study" at the end of this book is a list of books that I have found useful and interesting. It begins with books that are of general interest and then lists books that are especially relevant to each exercise. If you find yourself particularly intrigued with your response to a certain exercise, check the listings in the "Further Study" section. These resources will lead you to deeper explorations in the same area.

In the next section, "Suggestions for Group Work," I offer guidelines for using this book in a weekly study group.

Remember that your purpose is simply to practice self-reflection. Be kind and curious—and don't be surprised if you find yourself having fun.

Suggestions for Group Work

FOR MANY OF US, sharing our inner journeys helps break down the societal illusion that each of us is just "too weird for the world." Group work gives us the opportunity to both learn from each other and act as guides when we can. I encourage you to use this book to enhance your work with existing support circles, study groups, and classes; to find a friend with whom you can compare notes as you work through the book together; or to start a new group especially to share your "prayers to the moon." Here are some suggestions.

- By using the Almanac Route, your group will be doing the same exercises as other groups meeting through the year. Knowing that many other people are focusing on these exercises at the same time creates a subtle connection with others in this important inner work.

- Rotate the role of facilitator each week. Everyone should take a turn. The facilitator is responsible for keeping the group's focus on the week's exercise without discouraging helpful discussions that may range far wider than the exercise itself. The exercises are meant as a beginning point, not as an end in themselves.

- Agree to confidentiality of everything shared in your discussions to establish a safe environment where you can explore as deeply as you wish.

- Agree that this is not "group therapy." Individual issues that may benefit from special counseling will probably come up and can be identified, but members should not expect therapy from the group.

- Begin by going around the circle. Check in briefly to establish a connection with the present moment and with each other.

- Some possible questions to stimulate discussion might be: What did you observe this week that surprised you? What differences did you notice between your constructed selves and your essential self? What was your "take-home message" from the week's work? Some examples might be: "I tend to focus on the next task on my list rather than the one I'm doing at the moment," "I balance my energies everyday when I swim," "I measure my progress against what I think my ex-partner's expectations would be," and "When the moon is new, I feel excited and eager to take risks."

- Allow everyone equal time to talk.

- Respect each person's privacy: It is all right not to talk.

- End the session by having the facilitator read the next week's exercise aloud, but without group discussion or comment. Each person's unique interpretation and response should have an opportunity to develop during the week.

- If all agree, close by meditating together for a few moments, connecting with the other people who are working this book.

Each group will create its own style, so use these suggestions as a starting point and let your work together lead your group in its own special directions. Although I cannot answer letters personally, I am interested in hearing of your experiences with this book and encourage you to write me about them, c/o Escapadia Press, P.O. Box 5298, Atlanta, GA, 30307.

Key to the Nautilus Route

7. Personal Mail
36. Alone Time
44. Shadow Side
39. Moonstruck
24. Home Free
3. Sea of Crisis
27. Eclipse
23. Control
42. Ocean of Storms
31. Altar Ego
21. The Other You
15. Role Model
10. Breath
12. Back to Nature
4. Check In
41. Marsh of Sleep
46. Stop/Watch
30. Sea of Vapors

14. Waning Moon
9. Scrutiny
17. Repetition
51. Initiating Change
45. Marsh of Fog
2. List of Desires
34. The Daily Day
50. The Physical Plane
35. Integrity
11. Growing Pains
52. Ring-Pass-Not
16. Webpoints
19. Independent Study
5. Sea of Tranquility
25. Waxing Moon
18. Simple Pleasures
43. Weeding
38. Harvest Moon

48. Personal Map
40. Discipline
1. Lake of Dreams
28. Ebb and Flow
32. Full Moon
26. Nesting
13. Intuitrip
37. Sea of Nectar
22. Chinese Clue
49. Totem Story
33. Bay of Rainbows
6. New Moon
29. Moonlighting
8. Animal Guide
47. Old Friends
20. Full Circle

1. Lake of Dreams

DREAMS EMERGE FROM THE SUBCONSCIOUS, considered by many traditions to be the realm of the moon. Some cultures consider the dream world to be reality, valuing experiences in dreams far more than those in waking life. Children are encouraged to relate their dreams to parents each morning, looking for messages and lessons. Whatever your beliefs about dreams, they combine elements from our daily lives with the fantastic, offering us a glimpse beyond our preconceived notions into a realm where our minds are at play. This week, make an effort to remember your dreams and try to evoke special ones by forming a question or choosing a subject just before sleeping. Recall any dreams from the past that have lingered in your mind and speculate on their meanings here.

January 1–7

The moon is soundless;
it has no air to carry sound waves.

January 1–7

The full moon is a time of high energy and great sensitivity.

2. List of Desires

WHEN YOU KNOW WHAT YOU WANT, you notice opportunities to move toward your desires and recognize when you achieve them. Write a "list of desires" here, including both short- and long-term wishes, material items, professional accomplishments, local and global concerns, and immediate gratifications such as eating a meal in a favorite restaurant or reorganizing your work space. Do not limit yourself, but deeply inventory your desires. Come back to this entry several times this week after you have had a chance to consult your deeper self, and add anything you want. Make a note to review this list in three months, checking off desires you have fulfilled and adding new ones.

January 8–14

The Algonquin tribe called the full moon
of January the "Wolf Moon."

January 8–14

Moonrise occurs when the moon comes over
the earth's eastern horizon.

3. Sea of Crisis

A TRAP IS A DEVICE OR CONDITION that restricts movement. Sometimes you can be trapped by situations, habits, social customs, the prevailing views of your culture, or your own unwillingness to act. Usually, our traps are a combination of many things. I once felt trapped in an abusive relationship by my beliefs that I should stick with my partner "no matter what" and that leaving would mean I had failed. As my self-esteem increased, I realized that abuse was not acceptable in a loving relationship "no matter what" and I was able to leave. When have you felt trapped? Identify the different aspects of the trap, the parts you could not control, the roles you might have played in being trapped, and the ways you chose to handle the situation. Did you escape, or are you still constrained by the trap? Think of who or what might help you escape now and imagine ways you can avoid this trap in the future.

January 15–21

*The "seas" of the moon are formed
of ancient lava flows.*

January 15–21

A rille is a valley or small canyon
on the moon's surface.

4. Check In

PRACTICE CHECKING IN with your body, emotions, needs, and desires. Focusing only on the present moment, finish these sentences: "I feel _____; I need _____; I want _____." Try this several times daily until you feel comfortable pausing to assess your current mood and what contributes to it. This gentle, direct self-observation will connect you to your essential self. You may find the assignment more difficult than you expect, because most of us are not accustomed to paying close attention to our own "vital signs." Keep practicing.

January 22–28

Sanskrit, Greek, Latin, and Polynesian words
for spirit and mind are connected to the earliest
Indo-European words for moon and month.

January 22–28

*Menstrual cycles are generally the
length of the moon's cycle.*

5. Sea of Tranquility

BUTTERFLIES RUN ON SOLAR POWER. Cells in the design of their wings collect the warmth that powers their flight. When you see a butterfly at rest, perched on a flower, spreading its wings, it is said to be "basking," pausing to gather energy for future movement. How do you bask in your life? What do you do to restore your energy and vitality? Reading for pleasure, getting a massage, and walking in the woods are some of my favorites.

January 29–February 4

The Tewa tribe called the full moon of February the
"Moon When the Coyotes Are Frightened."

January 29–February 4

The moon is about 4.6 billion years old.

6. New Moon

MOST OF US USE NAMES GIVEN TO US BY OUR PARENTS. Some of us identify strongly with our given names, while others feel indifferent to or even disconnected from our names. List all your names, including nicknames used in the past and terms of endearment. How did you get these names? Which ones do you like the most? In some cultures, everyone chooses a secret power name, which can change through the years. Choose a name for yourself that evokes your current identity, that essential spirit moving in the world today. Try out different names here, describe their meanings, and select one by the end of the week. You can use a name you know or invent a new one. If you are satisfied with your given name, describe what it means to you.

February 5–11

The new moon occurs when the moon is directly between the earth and the sun.

February 5–11

The new moon is a time of dreams, vision, and magic.

7. Personal Mail

WRITE A LETTER TO SOMEONE RATHER DISTANT (geographically or emotionally), a friend you have not seen in a long time, or someone from whom you feel estranged. You may start the letter a number of times before you find the "voice" that feels comfortable and accurate to you. Keep your false starts and review them in a few days. What inner selves were speaking there? How would you characterize the voice you eventually chose to use in the letter? (You do not have to mail the letter.)

February 12–18

*Seeds are able to take in more moisture
during the full moon.*

February 12–18

Most ancient civilizations based their calendars on a lunar cycle.

8. Animal Guide

MANY CULTURES STUDY ANIMAL HABITS to understand essential truths about nature, the earth cycles and how to live in harmony with them. In some Native American religions, each animal is said to have specific healing "medicine" to share with human creatures. A glimpse of an animal, in reality or in dreams, is regarded as a sign to meditate on that animal's special qualities. Some Native American shamans practice "shape-shifting" trances in which they visit an animal's body for a time. What animals have you encountered lately? What kind of animal would you like to be? What qualities of this animal attract you? A sloth, for instance, notices things, does not get stressed out, eats lots of fruit, and spends days in sexual play. You might begin your entry using first person, "I am a deer. I run freely through the woods." This week, find an image of the animal you chose and place it at your bedside.

February 19–25

A new moon rises and sets with the sun.

February 19–25

An omen is a revelation from the moon.

9. Scrutiny

MOST CHOICES WE MAKE ARE AUTOMATIC AND UNCONSCIOUS. We choose to brush our teeth, to dress, and to have cereal for breakfast. Some choices—to make a phone call, to state an opinion, to work late—are made from a more conscious but perfunctory level, while others receive our obsessive attention, such as when we deliberate on a job change, or hesitate before asking someone for a date, or decide whether or not to spend a holiday with the family. This week, notice when you are making choices. Consider why you select certain ones for your conscious attention. List here some of the decisions you are aware of needing to make and during the week record others that come to your attention.

February 26—March 4

The moon is a symbol of connectedness.

February 26–March 4

*The diameter of the moon is less than
the width of the United States.*

10. Breath

TODAY, SPEND FIVE MINUTES SITTING COMFORTABLY with your eyes closed and notice your breath. To help focus, you may want to try counting your breaths. When a thought comes up, watch the thought and return your attention to your breath. Afterward, write in this journal for five minutes. On another day this week, prepare to meditate by writing in this journal for five minutes, then sit mindfully breathing. Which sequence do you like better? Why? Occasionally during the day, return your focus to your breath for a few moments. Appreciate how your body breathes for you when you are unaware.

March 5–11

Lunar energy is constantly affecting how we feel.

March 5–11

The surface temperature of the moon: 120° C during the day, −153° C at night.

11. Growing Pains

A COMMON WAY OF DEALING WITH PAINFUL MEMORIES, sorrow, or grief is denial. But such denial can extend far beyond specific painful incidents to affect our ability to feel other emotions such as joy, excitement, and satisfaction. This week, allow yourself to name aspects of your life that continue to hurt. You may simply want to list them. If you choose, select one and spend some time here describing the situation and its influence on your life. After you have completed this exercise, take note of what happens when you think of the situation.

March 12–18

*The San Juan tribe called the
full moon of March the "Lizard Moon."*

March 12–18

A full moon often means wet weather.

12. Back to Nature

THIS WEEK, SPEND ONE HOUR SITTING QUIETLY in a natural setting —a park or suburban neighborhood if you live in the city or a meadow, field, or mesa if you live in a rural area. Observe what is happening in the natural world. Describe what you experience as you become still. Do you feel a part of nature—or apart from it? Notice a particular plant or tree, scents, shadows and light, subtle colors and sounds. If possible, go back to the same spot several times this week and look for changes. Then, return in a month and look again.

March 19–25

At the vernal and autumn equinoxes,
the sun is directly over the equator.

March 19–25

*Easter, or Oestre, is the first Sunday following
the first full moon that occurs on or after
March 21, the spring equinox.*

13. Intuitrip

HAVE AN ADVENTURE THIS WEEK. Find several hours, if possible, and go somewhere you have never been before. Take provisions (sketchbook, journal, snack) but leave your expectations at home. On such a trip, allow your intuition to lead the way and notice when serendipity changes your path. Observe with the traveler's eye, appreciating the details of each moment as you might when you are on a trip. Bring home a souvenir and describe your adventure here. What happened that surprised you?

March 26–April 1

*A waxing crescent moon lags a few hours
behind the sun's rise and set.*

March 26–April 1

Experiencing the moon has been an important part
of the development of human consciousness.

14. Waning Moon

SHEDDING IS A NATURAL CONSEQUENCE OF GROWTH. Deer shed their antlers. Snakes shed their skins. Animals shed their fur. As humans, we shed our entire epidermal layer every twenty-nine and one-half days, the complete cycle of the moon; and we replace all the cells of our bodies every seven years. We are constantly letting go of the old as we create the new. But shedding outworn aspects of the self can be confusing or stressful as well as exhilarating and rewarding. Our new "skins" can feel tender and vulnerable until we become used to them. Even when we have outgrown them, the old ones, with their familiar scars and weatherworn bumps, often seem more comfortable. The need for a shedding might cause you to feel tense, cranky, or restless. Can you recall a recent shedding, one you either initiated or simply became aware of as it occurred? Describe the process, including how you knew when you were done. What do you need to shed now?

April 2–8

The waning moon is a left-hand crescent.

April 2–8

The waning moon is a time for finishing projects
and following through on ideas.

15. Role Model

ROLE MODELS ARE PEOPLE WE ADMIRE who have accomplished goals to which we aspire and live with integrity and dignity. Who are your current role models, and how are they similar to or different from those you had as a child? Describe what you admire about these people and why they are inspiring to you. What qualities do you share with them? If you cannot think of a role model, look for one this week. (The biography section of a bookstore or library may help you.) If you still cannot find a role model, create an imaginary one.

April 9–15

The Lakota Sioux tribes called the full moon of
April the "Moon of Grass Appearing."

April 9–15

In Polynesian belief, the dying moon journeyed to paradise, where it bathed in waters of immortality and, restored to vigor, returned in three days.

16. Webpoints

THE WEB OF YOUR CHOSEN FAMILY is made up of people with whom you feel secure, loved, respected, and accepted. These "webpoints" are special connections, relationships that encourage and inspire creative expression and may or may not include members of your birth family. Chosen family changes over time and circumstance. Who is in your chosen family today? List these people here, describing why you chose them. Consider having a family reunion with these special friends.

April 16–22

In ancient Egypt, the moon was
"mother of the universe."

April 16–22

The earth and moon orbit in a counterclockwise,
or "widdershins," direction.

17. Repetition

REPETITION IS A FORM OF CONDITIONING, a way we receive and incorporate information. This week, notice repeated messages that you receive, such as traffic signals, advertising slogans, government policies, compliments from friends and associates, and internal voices of criticism or encouragement. What information does each message convey? What messages are you repeating to yourself? Which ones do you use intentionally, and which ones are absorbed unconsciously? Think of an affirming message, such as "I have plenty of time to accomplish my work," and repeat it frequently to yourself this week. Post it on the bathroom mirror and the refrigerator. Notice any effect this has and return here to record your findings.

April 23–29

Hecate was the Greek goddess of the dark moon.

April 23–29

The moon rotates around its axis once
every twenty-nine and a half days.

18. Simple Pleasures

WHAT BRINGS YOU PLEASURE? Make a list here of "simple pleasures," those small things that delight and surprise you, cause you to pause and enjoy the moment: a peaking blossom, a cloud splashed by the setting sun, a letter from a friend, unexpected praise or recognition. This week, notice feelings of pleasure and when they occur. Describe one of these feelings in elaborate detail here, remembering all the sensory aspects you experienced: smell, taste, sound, touch, sight, and those subtle perceptions on intuitive, spiritual, and psychic levels.

April 30–May 6

Moondogs, *or* mock moons, *are pale*
images off to the moon's side that
are caused by humidity.

April 30–May 6

A lack of moonlight may result in poor health.

19. Independent Study

EDUCATIONAL EXPERIENCES THAT HAPPEN OUTSIDE A CLASSROOM are different from the "formal" education of schools and other institutions. Describe independent learning experiences that have influenced you, such as caring for an aging parent, recovering from a physical injury, or a group project such as a political campaign or a neighborhood garden. List the skills and wisdom you gained from these experiences. What current involvments are part of your independent education? What else would you like to learn, and how might you go about learning it?

May 7–13

*The Taos tribe called the full moon of May
the "Corn-Planting Moon."*

May 7–13

The moon keeps the same side always facing the earth.

20. Full Circle

THIS WEEK, WEATHER PERMITTING, find an opportunity to lie down on the earth. For a few minutes or as long as you like, allow yourself to stare at the sky, to watch the clouds, stars, moon, or sunlight, while you feel the earth solidly beneath you. Feeling your full connection to the planet, breathe and center yourself on the earth. If you cannot be outside, lie down on the floor or even on your bed. Picture the house you are in, its foundations deep in the ground, and the earth that supports you. Some people believe that the earth itself is a living entity. Ask it for a message and return here to record what you hear.

May 14–20

*The waxing moon is a time of increase,
rising energy, and new beginnings.*

May 14–20

*The moon completes one earth orbit every
twenty-nine and a half days.*

21. The Other You

IMAGINE YOU HAVE A TWIN WHO IS YOUR OPPOSITE in personality, temperament, talents, and preferences. Like you, your twin will have strengths and weaknesses. Describe this person in as much detail as you can. In a few days, after observing your own qualities and thinking about their opposites, come back and refine your description.

May 21–27

A blue moon is a full moon that occurs twice in the same month.

May 21–27

A first-quarter moon is visible half the day and half the night.

22. Chinese Clue

THE I CHING, OR BOOK OF CHANGES, is an ancient Chinese philosophical system that has sixty-four messages describing different phases of growth and awareness. Sit quietly for a moment, clear your mind, and breathe evenly. Choose a number between one and sixty-four. Record the number here. This week, find a guidebook to the I Ching in the library, a friend's house, a bookstore or on your own bookshelf. Read the entry that corresponds to your chosen number and return here to record your message.

May 28–June 3

*The oldest lunar calendar still in use has been used
in China since 2698 B.C.E.*

May 28–June 3

A waxing gibbous moon lags eight to ten hours behind the sun's rise and set.

23. Control

ALL CULTURES USE SOME FORM OF SOCIAL CONTROL to maintain specific kinds of "order." Some forms are obvious, such as segregating the races or physical torture, while other forms operate on a more subtle level, such as censorship of the press, selective enforcement of laws, or stereotypes in advertising. What kinds of social control does your culture use? Think of the last time you felt controlled by such societal structures and describe the control method here. Do you believe it is necessary for order? Imagine several other ways we might use to encourage social harmony.

June 4–10

*The San Ildefonso tribe called the full moon
of June the "Flower Moon."*

June 4–10

*A full moon rises at about sunset and
sets at about sunrise.*

24. Home Free

I REMEMBER FEELING A SPECIAL SENSE OF SAFETY as a child when I fell asleep with my siblings in the backseat of the car as my parents drove us home. Now that I am an adult and a city dweller, that feeling has become more elusive. What does safety mean to you? When do you feel completely safe and at peace? Describe the last time you experienced these feelings and what contributed to your sense of well-being. If you cannot recall such a time, imagine a situation that might evoke feelings of safety and describe the circumstances. Notice when you feel safe this week.

June 11–17

In France, le moment de la lune *is
the name given to menstruation.*

June 11–17

*In many ancient cultures, pregnancy was
believed to be caused by the moon.*

25. Waxing Moon

HAVE YOU EVER FELT that there just were not enough hours in the day? Imagine that there are five more hours in every day, hours during which you feel alert, rested, and happy. Assuming that all your responsibilities and obligations for the day have been met, how will you choose to spend these extra hours? Find an hour or two this week to spend as you have described.

June 18–24

The waxing moon is a right-hand crescent.

June 18–24

The summer solstice, when the sun is at its most northern point, marks the longest day of the year.

26. Nesting

MOST OF US WILL HAVE MANY HOMES in the course of our lives. Our earliest home was made for us, but as we grow older, we begin to make our own. Sometimes we have more than one home at a time, and often we can feel at home in odd places. Beyond shelter and warmth, what does "home" mean to you? When and where do you feel "at home"? Describe various homes you have had in the past. When you establish a new one, how do you create the sense of home? Do you need a lot of space, a particular kind of light, books, a cozy kitchen, pictures on the walls? Have you ever felt homeless? You might begin your entry here: "Home is _____."

June 25–July 1

Astrologically, the moon describes our emotional
foundations formed in childhood.

June 25–July 1

*A waning gibbous moon precedes the sun's
rise and set by eight to ten hours.*

27. Eclipse

MANY OF OUR MOST INFLUENTIAL BELIEFS AND IDEAS were formed
when we were children imitating our parents or other caretaking adults.
If unexamined, these childhood impressions can act as masks over our actual
feelings in the moment and can continue to direct our choices. Describe
your childhood caretakers here, noting especially any strong opinions you
remember them expressing in words or actions. Try to identify your
similarities to and differences from the beliefs and opinions of your caretakers.
Look for the parental masks over your current thoughts and feelings and
reconsider any outdated beliefs.

Lunar eclipses are caused when the earth's shadow falls on the moon.

July 2–8

Lunar eclipses always occur during the full moon.

28. Ebb and Flow

PROCRASTINATION IS A SIGNAL OF BLOCKED ENERGY, often triggered by a sense of premonition or dread. What are you procrastinating about this week? Describe this situation here. Examine the reasons you might be putting something off and list the different options you have in order to accomplish the task. Think of one more option and then make a decision to initiate action to complete the chore. Name your first step. Make an effort to unblock the energy channel this week by taking the step you have named. Return here to describe what happens.

July 9–15

The San Juan tribes called the full moon
of July the "Ripe Moon."

July 9–15

A last-quarter moon is visible half the day and half the night.

29. Moonlighting

IMAGINE THAT YOU HAVE BEEN INVITED to teach a class at a school for life experiences. Drawing from areas of passion, expertise, and skill in your own life, you may teach anything you want in any manner that you wish. "Roadtripping: Cross-Country Driving for Fun and Adventure," "Creating a Sacred Space in Your Home," and "Surprise Packages: Making Eggrolls, Dolmas, Tamales, and Other Wrapped Food" are in my own curriculum. Write the course description for the school catalog here.

July 16–22

*Superstitious Christians sometimes refused to
sleep where moonlight might touch them.*

July 16–22

*A waning crescent precedes the sun's rise
and set by a few hours.*

30. Sea of Vapors

LYING IS A WAY TO CONTROL INFORMATION: If I lie to you, I have information that you do not have, and I am supplying false information that you believe to be true. Until the lie is discovered, the liar is in a power-over position. Have you ever found out that someone you trusted lied to you? Have you ever suspected that social institutions of, for example, the government, medicine, advertising, or the military—are lying? Many of our personal lies are habitual, often unintentional, disguised as tactfulness, silence, or a desire to appear "appropriate." Being careful not to judge yourself, gently observe your interactions this week and look for an instance when you choose to lie. Examine the situation to identify your motive, then imagine how telling the truth would change what happened.

July 23–29

*A total solar eclipse occurs when the moon
completely blocks the sun from the earth.*

July 23–29

In central Asia, it is thought that the moon is the Goddess's
mirror, reflecting everything in the world.

31. Altar Ego

A SHRINE IS AN INTENTIONAL GATHERING OF OBJECTS to which we assign meaning or power. Although generally associated with religious practice, shrines appear in our domestic environment, too. Sometimes we create them; other times they assemble by accident—snapshots on the refrigerator, souvenirs from a journey displayed on a shelf, even a growing pile of laundry. Shrines express our inner process in tangible form. They draw our attention and focus our concentration. Look for your shrines this week, in your home and work space. Describe what they look like and speculate on their meaning. Now, begin a shrine. Choose a spot you encounter frequently and place an object or image there, something with special meaning for you or that you simply like. Find other "power objects" to add to your shrine as the week continues.

July 30–August 5

*The first-quarter moon is 20 percent brighter
than the last-quarter moon.*

July 30–August 5

Modern birthday cakes come from the Greek custom
of honoring the monthly birthday of Artemis,
the moon, with lighted full-moon cakes.

32. Full Moon

THINK OF THREE PERSONAL ACHIEVEMENTS and list them here. Choose one and describe it in detail as if you were writing a letter to tell your good news to a friend. Practice bragging a bit, remembering that this friend enjoys sharing your happiness and delights in your achievements. With another one, write your account of it in third person: "In less than a year, Kay learned the complete long-form of t'ai chi, a sixty-four-movement martial-art sequence used in the Orient for maintaining flexibility and agility. She went to class every week and practiced the form at least twice a week. Her teacher said she was very good and offered her lessons in 'push-hands,' a partner form of t'ai chi."

August 6–12

*The Lakota Sioux tribes called the full moon of August
the "Moon When Cherries Turn Black."*

August 6–12

At its brightest point, the full moon gives off about .02 footcandles of light.

33. Bay of Rainbows

PEAK EXPERIENCES HAVE BEEN DESCRIBED as moments of uncommon clarity, insight, energy, and well-being. Sometimes they are associated with dramatic or unusual circumstances—for example, hiking the Grand Canyon or doing civil disobedience as a political action. At other times commonplace moments fully attended trigger peak experiences, such as watching your child sleep or eating a peach that is perfectly ripe. These incidents are glimpses of our essence and often carry a powerful message. Describe your most recent peak experience, with as much sensory detail as possible. What did you learn: What was the "take-home message"? If you do not recall a peak experience, imagine having one and describe your adventure here.

August 13–19

Moonbows, like rainbows, occur when light from the moon is refracted through water droplets, usually when the moon is full.

August 13–19

Sioux Indians called the moon the
"Old Woman Who Never Dies."

34. The Daily Day

ALTHOUGH MANY OF OUR HABITS ARE HELPFUL, we tend to lose contact with our bodies when we are lost in routine. This week, choose three daily habits—brushing your teeth, driving the car, and eating a meal, for example—and experiment with slowing down, paying attention to your body as you do. Brush your teeth at half speed one morning, drive slightly under the speed limit on your way home from work, or chew each bite twenty-five times at dinner one night. Do you feel tension in your body? If so, take several deep breaths and relax the tense spots. Describe the results of your experiment here and practice applying this mindfulness in other areas of your routine.

August 20–26

The weather tends to change at new and full moons,
with the largest amount of rainfall occurring
three to five days after the full moon.

August 20–26

When the moon looks red, expect rain.

35. Integrity

ONE DEFINITION OF INTEGRITY IS "when the inner voice has the upper hand." Another is "walking what you talk." Integrity implies consistency between intuition and practice, a wholeness and harmony between principle and action, belief and behavior. How would you define integrity? Name five people you feel have strong integrity. Now recall a time you faced a challenge to your integrity—for example, when your boss asked you to alter a report to make him look better or when a co-worker was mistakenly criticized for an error that you made. How did you respond to the situation? Do you feel that your integrity was intact? What did you learn about yourself and your beliefs through this experience?

August 27–September 2

The moon's light will control ovulation of a woman
who lives in only natural light.

August 27–September 2

Europe comes from the Greek europa,
meaning "full moon."

36. Alone Time

SOLITUDE IS DIFFERENT FROM LONELINESS. When you choose to spend
time alone, you are electing to focus your attention on your own process.
You are paying attention to your self the way you would a best friend or
cherished lover. Yet many of us fear solitude. When we find ourselves alone,
we fill up the time and space with activities that pull our attention outward.
Next time you start aimlessly flipping television channels or making idle
phone calls, pause and check in with yourself, focusing your attention inward.
What is it that you really want and need in this time? This week, make a date
with yourself to spend an hour alone, writing in your journal, meditating, or
doing some other reflective activity. Protect your privacy by unplugging
the phone or putting a "do not disturb" sign on your door. Observe your
responses and record them here.

September 3–9

The Nez Perce tribes called the full moon of September
the "Salmon-Spawning Time."

September 3–9

The moon is slightly egg shaped, not round.

37. Sea of Nectar

DESCRIBE WHAT BRINGS YOU EROTIC PLEASURE. If you have difficulty writing about this, just sit for a moment and think about it. Advertising, religion, family upbringing, and other cultural forces give us many mixed messages about sexual behavior, and our understanding of our sexual selves is often confused. When you next feel sexual excitement, notice the sequence of events and the particular quality of the moment—an aroma, a touch, the memory of a dream, a smile. Remember, too, that eroticism is not limited to sexual exchanges. Working with clay, planting a garden, or bodysurfing in the ocean may also be exciting and erotic. Study without judgment your responses to sensual pleasure, simply noticing what you like and do not like, and list your pleasures here.

September 10–16

The dark moon is a time of love magic, metamorphosis,
wonder working, and medicinal healing,
according to the ancient Greeks.

September 10–16

A wet moon is a low crescent,
like a cup holding water.

38. Harvest Moon

TAKE TIME TO NOTICE AREAS OF ABUNDANCE IN YOUR LIFE. Often scarcity, or the fear of scarcity, grabs our attention with urgency and crisis. Abundance is quiet, a presence that supports and nurtures us without demands. We may not realize the power that is available to us from abundance because of its lack of urgency. Your health, your chosen family, your training and experience, and your home are all areas that may give you consistent nurture through abundance. Explore the concept and experience of abundance in your life as you move through this week. List the areas here then choose one area and describe how it influences your choices.

September 17–23

The moon affects water: tides, our bodily fluids,
and the sap in plants.

September 17–23

Neap tide is the lowest high tide
of the lunar month.

39. Moonstruck

THIS WEEK, EXPLORE YOUR IDEALISM by designing a utopian society where everything is as it should be—according to you! Some areas to consider: how to make agreements and resolve conflict, guidelines for behavior, community principles, systems for communication, housing, and the economy. You might borrow from existing cultures, creating a "bill of rights" or "twelve steps" as well as inventing new values and forms that incorporate your own ideals. Do not forget to include fun and pleasure and allow you imagination full rein. As you construct your utopia, study the culture in which you live now, noting what you would retain and what you would change. Here is how I began: I have named my ideal society Escapadia, where we live in small, self-governing communities. We live close to the earth, eating what we grow and trading skills, tools, and art with other communities. Violence is forbidden and nearly forgotten. We use computer technology to participate in global efforts, but our main concerns are listening to the earth, communicating with other creatures, and enjoying the beauties of this planet. Country line-dancing and two-stepping are national pastimes. . . .

September 24–30

*To be moonstruck in ancient cultures
was to be chosen by the Goddess.*

September 24–30

The moon was the special deity of women during the Renaissance,
when it was said that if a woman wanted anything she should
not ask God but should pray instead to the moon.

40. Discipline

AN ARTIST ONCE SAID that "discipline is remembering what you want." What do you want that inspires your conscientious work, your devotion? Discipline can be obtained by punishment and coercion or by consistent guidance and positive reinforcement. I used to motivate myself to write by waiting until the last minute before a deadline, deliberately creating stressful crisis energy to get myself going. Now I am experimenting with a gentler pace, developing a plan and a time line early on, allowing me to devote full attention to each step. Study your habits this week to discover how you discipline yourself and describe your methods here.

October 1–7

The Sumerians believed that destinies
were fixed at the new moon.

October 1–7

*Physiologically, the moon governs the
balance of fluids in the body.*

41. Marsh of Sleep

WHILE I KNOW THAT PLASTIC BAGS TAKE HUNDREDS OF YEARS to disintegrate, I continue to use them in my trash cans every week, even though I am deeply concerned about the future of the planet. The ability to hold contradictory beliefs in the mind simultaneously is called "cognitive dissonance" and is a common response to problems that seem overwhelming, such as the destruction of the environment or the threat of nuclear annihilation. Look for your contradictory beliefs this week, describe them here, and imagine what would change about your behavior if you acknowledged them.

October 8–14

The Algonquin tribes called the full moon
of October the "Hunter's Moon."

October 8–14

From the earth, the moon appears to be
the same size as the sun.

42. Ocean of Storms

ANGER DRAWS A BOUNDARY, MAKES A STAND. When we get angry, we are expressing a limit and acknowledging a violation. Our anger says, "This violation is unacceptable." What we get angry about often illuminates our beliefs, values, and sense of entitlement. Although taking anger out on other people is inappropriate, feeling and expressing anger are vital to our well-being. When was the last time you felt angry? What were the circumstances or the issues involved? Did you express your feelings? What forms do you allow your anger to take?

October 15–21

Early Christians named Roman moon worshipers
lunatics *and thought them mad.*

October 15–21

In central Asia, it is said that the moon's reflection
on water is a remedy for nervous hysteria.

43. Weeding

DEFENESTRATION MEANS to "throw an object or a person out of the window." When we practice defenestration, we identify elements in our lives that are harmful or discouraging to us and oust them from our sphere of immediate influence. Like weeding a garden, this is a necessary habit to cultivate as we grow and change. For instance, I no longer see films that include gratuitous violence, especially male violence against women, because I do not want to reinforce acceptance of those behaviors in my own mind with powerful cinematic images. Examine your current situation and list the candidates for defenestration. Describe how they affect your life. How might you lessen their influence or eliminate them?

October 22–28

*In ancient cultures, most women menstruated at the new moon;
they separated from the nonmenstruating tribe to spend
time alone together during their "moon time."*

October 22–28

*Earliest human concepts of periodicity came from
observing the moon and its correlation to
the menstrual cycle and tidal changes.*

44. Shadow Side

THE MOON'S SHADOW SIDE NEVER FACES THE EARTH. Like the moon, we all have mysterious aspects of our personalities and past experiences, aspects we choose not to share with others. Our shadow side might include vulnerabilities, fantasies, and eccentricities—for example, a secret ambition to be a writer, an unrequited love, a penchant for collecting rocks, a fear of heights, or a belief in astrology. As our trust in a friend grows, we may cautiously reveal our shadow side or keep this realm of ourselves private. Whatever we choose, these aspects continue to influence our relationships and our self-regard. Visit your shadow side this week, and—for your own benefit—chart the terrain: Walk through your private realm and describe what you encounter there.

October 29–November 4

*The shadow side of the moon is said to bear
the creative seeds of the unconscious.*

October 29–November 4

Many ancient cultures, seeing the moon as the land of the dead and the unborn, believed that souls returned to the moon to await reincarnation.

45. Marsh of Fog

GHOSTS ARE HAUNTING MEMORIES of unresolved relationships. A ghost might be a physical space, a person (alive or dead), an abandoned project, an unexpressed feeling, or a road not taken. When we feel incomplete about a relationship or situation, we often remain attached through longing, resentment, or anger that keeps us from truly letting go and moving on in life. Name some ghosts in your life and why you feel unresolved about them. Choose one and imagine a peaceful resolution: What does it look like? What does resolution involve? Describe steps you might take to initiate completion and consider how your feelings would change if this ghost were put to rest.

November 5–11

The Cheyenne tribes called the full moon of
November the "Freezing Moon."

November 5–11

World mythologies portray the waxing, full, and waning moons as maiden, mother, and crone.

46. Stop/Watch

WHETHER WE WATCH TELEVISION OR NOT, it is a contemporary companion of questionable but undeniably strong effect on individuals and on our culture at large. Television is known to influence our concentration span, our shopping habits, and our dreams. If you usually watch television as part of your normal routine, stop for this week. If you are not in the habit of watching television, this week watch it for two hours per day. (This is much less than the national average!) If you do not have a television, make arrangements with a friend who has one to spend several hours daily watching it. Notice your reactions, how this experiment changes your awareness and your habits, and record them here. Examine and characterize your ongoing relationship with television—for instance, is it an intimate partner, a casual acquaintance, a propaganda device, or a relaxation appliance?

November 12–18

A solar eclipse is always followed or preceded
by a lunar eclipse within fourteen days.

November 12–18

For centuries, planting and harvesting
have been guided by the moon.

47. Old Friends

REMEMBER BACK TO YOUR CHILD SELF, to a time when you believed
in fairies, elves, "imaginary" friends, or other playful spirits. What were their
names? Where did you see them? What did they look like? What powers
did they have? Some people believe throughout their lives in angels, devas,
guides, saints, and other protective spirits as spiritual companions. If you have
such a presence in your life, describe it here. If not, invent one!

The moon rules the lunar realms of memory and the unconscious.

November 19–25

Moonset occurs when the moon drops over the earth's western horizon.

48. Personal Map

AN OLD SAYING GOES, "If you don't know where you're going, any road will take you there." When you have a specific destination, however, you can select the path leading in the direction of your goal. Having a destination helps you identify opportunities, avoid obvious obstacles, and clarify your priorities. Create your own personal map this week by naming three things you want to accomplish within the next year. Be realistic as well as challenging: Naming impossible tasks merely serves to demoralize you. Last year, my goals were to finish writing this book, to cultivate my wildness, and to contact lost friends. Hone your goals to things that will cause you to stretch, to reach beyond your known capacity, while allowing you to reasonably fulfill your expectations. Over the year, come back to this page and check your progress toward meeting your pledges.

November 26–December 2

The moon's cycle shows us continual transition,
where each step is equally valuable.

November 26–December 2

*The weather during the fourth and fifth days after the new
moon is an indicator for the coming lunar month.*

49. Totem Story

MOST PEOPLE HAVE SIGNATURE CHILDHOOD STORIES, those personal tales that are repeated year after year by family members or close friends. These stories become our own legends and can act as snapshots of our personalities. These vivid imprints usually have both positive and negative implications and directly affect our self-esteem and self-image. My parents were fond of relating an incident that occurred when I was about two years old, when I insisted on taking a bath without their assistance, informing them, "I'll do it me-self!" This declaration came to signify a stubbornness— and a distinctive independence!—that my parents noticed early in my life. Tell one of your "totem" stories here and describe what personal qualities it suggests.

December 3–9

The Wisham tribes called the full moon of December
"Her Winter Houses Moon."

December 3–9

In Latin, the word mens *means both*
"moon" and "mind."

50. The Physical Plane

NOTICE HOW YOU ARE FEELING IN YOUR BODY as you read this exercise. Are you holding tension in different areas? Where? Are you comfortable in your chair, in your clothes, with the temperature of the room? What is competing for your attention? List these observations and then spend ten minutes sitting with your eyes closed, breathing evenly, and relaxing your muscles. During the week, slow down your habitual movements and notice your physical sensations. Be in your body. When you pull on your sock, pay attention to your foot. How does this practice affect you?

December 10–16

Astrologically, the moon is said to govern
the general conditions of health.

December 10–16

Women who live near the equator tend to menstruate during full moon.

51. Initiating Change

SOMETIMES CHANGE HAPPENS TO US. At other times we initiate it.
List changes that have been imposed on you, such as the death of a parent
or community water rationing. Now name changes you have initiated, such
as getting training in a special field or accepting a leadership role in a community project. What elements of your life would you like to change and
how? List them here and then imagine the changes you would prefer for each
area. Choose one and describe the steps you might take to initiate the process
of change. For example, I would like to deal with money more clearly. Steps
might include balancing my checkbook promptly, recording tax-deductible
receipts each week, creating a written budget, and making a plan for paying
off my credit cards.

December 17–23

The winter solstice, when the sun is at its most southern point, marks the longest night of the year.

December 17–23

The moon is constantly changing.

52. Ring-Pass-Not

BEFORE THE INVENTION OF THE TELESCOPE, human beings understood the universe through the limitations of unaided human sight. Saturn was the last visible planet, its orbit creating what early astronomers called the "ring-pass-not." This term has come to symbolize the limit of the known world at any given point in time. Now, with the discovery of Pluto and the possibility of even more distant planets, humans have an expanded notion of the celestial ring-pass-not. Take this image into your personal sphere. After the kids are grown, moving to a different place, finishing school, changing careers—what are your own rings-pass-not, those aspects of your life beyond which you cannot see?

December 24–31

Spring tide is the highest tide of month,when

earth, sun, and moon are aligned.

December 24–31

In Finnish lore, the moon goddess Luonnatar
brought the World Egg from the sea.

Further Study

The following books helped me to construct the Almanac and Nautilus sequences and to collect moon facts. They served as general resources in the conception of this book, along with the books cited for specific exercises.

Arrien, Angeles. *The Tarot Handbook: Practical Applications of Ancient Visual Symbols*. Sonoma, CA: Arcus, 1987.

Budapest, Zsuzsanna E. *The Grandmother of Time: A Women's Book of Celebrations, Spells, and Sacred Objects for Every Month of the Year*. San Francisco: Harper & Row, 1990.

Daly, Mary. *Gyn/Ecology: The Metaethics of Radical Feminism*. Boston: Beacon, 1978, 1990.

—. *Pure Lust: Elemental Feminist Philosophy*. Boston: Beacon, 1984.

Lanning, Lee, Nett Hart, and other word weavers. *Ripening/Dreaming/Awakening: Almanacs of Lesbian Lore and Vision*. Minneapolis: Word Weavers, 1981, 1983, 1987.

Long, Kim. *The Moon Book*. Boulder, CO: Johnson, 1988.

River, Lindsay, and Sally Gillespie. *The Knot of Time: Astrology and the Female Experience*. New York: Harper & Row, 1987.

Introduction: Evoking the Essential Self

Berends, Polly Berrien. *Coming to Life: Traveling the Spiritual Path in Everyday Life*. San Francisco: Harper & Row, 1990.

Hoagland, Sarah Lucia. *Lesbian Ethics: Toward New Value*. Palo Alto, CA: Institute of Lesbian Studies, 1988.

Schideler, Mary McDermott. *In Search of the Spirit*. New York: Ballantine, 1985.

Sjöo, Monica, and Barbara Mor. *The Great Cosmic Mother: Rediscovering the Religion of the Earth.* San Francisco: Harper & Row, 1987.

1. Lake of Dreams

LaBerge, Stephen. *Lucid Dreaming: The Power of Being Awake and Aware in Your Dreams.* New York: Ballantine, 1985.

2. List of Desires

Sher, Barbara. *Wishcraft: How to Get What You Really Want.* New York: Ballantine, 1979.

3. Sea of Crisis

Sanford, Linda Tschirhart, and Mary Ellen Donovan. *Women and Self-Esteem: Understanding and Improving the Way We Think and Feel about Ourselves.* New York: Penguin, 1985.

4. Check In

Butler, Pamela. *Talking to Yourself: Learning the Language of Self-Affirmation.* San Francisco: Harper & Row, 1991. Revised edition.

Gendlin, Eugene. *Focusing.* New York: Bantam, 1981.

5. Sea of Tranquility

Grudin, Robert. *Time and the Art of Living.* New York: Ticknor & Fields, 1988.

6. New Moon

Hagan, Kay Leigh. *Internal Affairs: A Journalkeeping Workbook for Self-Intimacy.* San Francisco: Harper & Row, 1990.

7. Personal Mail

Adams, Kathleen. *Journal to the Self: Twenty-Two Paths to Personal Growth.* New York: Warner, 1990.

8. Animal Guide

Sams, Jamie, and David Carson. *Medicine Cards: The Discovery of Power through the Ways of Animals.* Santa Fe, NM: Bear, 1988.

9. Scrutiny

Palmer, Helen. *The Enneagram*. San Francisco: Harper & Row, 1988.

10. Breath

Macbeth, Jessica. *Moon Over Water: Meditation Made Clear with Techniques for Beginners and Initiates*. Bath, England: Gateway, 1990.

Kingsolver, Barbara. *Animal Dreams*. New York: Harper & Row, 1990.

11. Growing Pains

Macy, Joanna Rogers. *Despair and Personal Power in the Nuclear Age*. Philadelphia: New Society, 1983.

12. Back to Nature

Seed, John, Joanna Rogers Macy, Pat Fleming, and Arne Naess. *Thinking Like a Mountain: Towards a Council of All Beings*. Philadelphia: New Society, 1988.

13. Intuitrip

Davison, Robyn. *Tracks*. New York: Pantheon, 1983.

14. Waning Moon

Kingsolver, Barbara. *Animal Dreams*. New York: Harper & Row, 1990.

15. Role Model

Spender, Dale. *Women of Ideas and What Men Have Done to Them*. London: Thorsons, 1991.

16. Webpoints

Lindsey, Karen. *Friends as Family*. Boston: Beacon, 1981.

Raymond, Janice G. *A Passion for Friends: Toward a Philosophy of Female Affection*. Boston: Beacon, 1986.

17. Repetition

Solomon, Jack. *The Signs of Our Time: The Secret Meanings of Everyday Life*. New York: Harper & Row, 1988.

Tart, Charles. *Waking Up: Overcoming the Obstacles to Human Potential.* Boston: Shambhala, 1987.

18. Simple Pleasures

Hanh, Thich Nhat. *The Miracle of Mindfulness: A Manual on Meditation.* Boston: Beacon, 1987.

19. Independent Study

Gross, Ronald. *Independent Scholar's Handbook: How to Turn Your Interest in Any Subject into Expertise.* Reading, MA: Addison-Wesley, 1982.

20. Full Circle

Nichols, John. *The Sky's the Limit: A Defense of the Earth.* New York: Norton, 1990.

21. The Other You

Herrera, Hayden. *Frida: A Biography of Frida Kahlo.* New York: Harper & Row, 1984.

Stoltenberg, John. *Refusing to Be a Man.* Portland, OR: Breitenbush, 1989.

22. Chinese Clue

Anthony, Carol K. *A Guide to the I Ching.* Stow, MA: Anthony, 1988.

23. Control

Atwood, Margaret. *The Handmaid's Tale.* New York: Fawcett, 1986.

Katz, Judy H. *White Awareness: Handbook for Anti-Racism Training.* Norman: Univ. of Oklahoma Press, 1987.

Key, Wilson Bryan. *Subliminal Seduction.* New York: NAL, 1978.

24. Home Free

Delacoste, Frederique, and Felice Newman. *Fight Back: Feminist Resistance to Male Violence.* Minneapolis, MN: Cleis, 1981.

Dworkin, Andrea. *Letters from a War Zone.* New York: Dutton, 1989.

Gearhart, Sally. *The Wanderground.* Boston: Alyson, 1984.

25. Waxing Moon

Sinetar, Marcia. *Do What You Love, The Money Will Follow*. New York: Dell, 1989.

26. Nesting

Woolf, Virginia. *A Room of One's Own*. New York: Harcourt Brace, 1989.

27. Eclipse

Conroy, Pat. *Prince of Tides*. New York: Bantam, 1986.

28. Ebb and Flow

Bailey, Linda J. *How to Get Going When You Can Barely Get Out of Bed: Every Woman's Handbook for Dealing with Depression and Frustration*. New York: Prentice-Hall, 1984.

29. Moonlighting

Hart, Mickey, with Jay Stevens. *Drumming at the Edge of Magic*. San Francisco: HarperCollins, 1990.

30. Sea of Vapors

Hagan, Kay Leigh. *The Invisible Obvious: Fugitive Information #3*. Atlanta: Escapadia, 1990. (Available from author at P.O. Box 5298, Atlanta, GA 30307.)

Penelope, Julia. *Speaking Freely: Unlearning the Lies of the Father's Tongues*. New York: Pergamon, 1990.

31. Altar Ego

Hagan, Kay Leigh. *Internal Affairs: A Journalkeeping Workbook for Self-Intimacy*. San Francisco: Harper & Row, 1990.

32. Full Moon

Shekerjian, Denise. *Uncommon Genius: How Great Ideas Are Born*. New York: Viking, 1990.

33. Bay of Rainbows

Steiner, Ralph, and Caroline Steiner, eds. *In Spite of Everything, Yes*. Albuquerque: Univ. of New Mexico Press, 1986.

Tart, Charles. *Open Mind, Discriminating Mind: Reflections on Human Possibilities*. San Francisco: Harper & Row, 1990.

34. The Daily Day

Hanh, Thich Nhat. *Being Peace*. Berkeley, CA: Parallax, 1987.

Langer, Ellen J. *Mindfulness*. Reading, MA: Addison-Wesley, 1989.

35. Integrity

Daly, Mary. *Pure Lust: Elemental Feminist Philosophy*. Boston: Beacon, 1984.

36. Alone Time

Adair, Margo. *Working Inside Out: Tools for Change—Applied Mediation for Intuitive Problem Solving*. Berkeley, CA: Wingbow, 1984.

37. Sea of Nectar

Brossard, Nicole. *Sous La Langue (Under Tongue)*. Prince George Island: Gynergy, 1987.

Hawthorne, Susan, and Jenny Pausacher. *Moments of Desire: Sex and Sensuality by Australian Feminist Writers*. Victoria, British Columbia: Penguin, 1989.

38. Harvest Moon

Anderson, Margaret C. *My Thirty Years' War, the Fiery Fountains, the Strange Necessity*. New York: Horizon, 1970.

Reynolds, David K. *Pools of Lodging for the Moon: Strategy for a Positive Life Style*. New York: Morrow, 1989.

39. Moonstruck

Frye, Marilyn. *The Politics of Reality: Essays in Feminist Theory*. Freedom, CA: Crossing, 1983.

Piercy, Marge. *Woman on the Edge of Time*. New York: Fawcett, 1985.

Rochrlich, Ruby and Elaine Baruch. *Women in Search of Utopia: Mavericks and Mythmakers*. New York: Schocken, 1984.

40. Discipline

Atchity, Kenneth. *A Writer's Time: A Guide to the Creative Process, from Vision through Revision*. New York: Norton, 1986.

Levin, Jennifer. *Waterdancer*. New York: Pocket Books, 1982.

41. Marsh of Sleep

Goleman, Daniel. *Vital Lies, Simple Truths: The Psychology of Self-Deception*. New York: Simon & Schuster, 1985.

42. Ocean of Storms

Lerner, Harriet. *The Dance of Anger*. New York: Harper & Row, 1985.

43. Weeding

Field, Joanna. *A Life of One's Own*. Los Angeles: Tarcher, 1981.

44. Shadow Side

Shivers, Louise. *Here to Get My Baby Out of Jail*. New York: Random, 1983.

45. Marsh of Fog

Hansen, Renee. *Take Me to the Underground*. Freedom, CA: Crossing, 1990.

46. Stop/Watch

Mander, Jerry. *Four Arguments for the Elimination of Television*. New York: Morrow, 1978.

Nelson, Joyce. *The Perfect Machine: TV in the Nuclear Age*. Toronto: Between the Lines, 1987.

47. Old Friends

Berger, Barbara Helen. *When the Sun Rose*. New York: Putnam, 1986.

Norton, Mary. *The Borrowers*. New York: Harcourt Brace, 1981.

48. Personal Map

Koberg, Don, and Jim Bagnall. *The Universal Traveler: A Soft-Systems Guide to Creativity, Problem-Solving, and the Process of Reaching Goals*. Los Altos, CA: Kaufmann, 1976.

49. Totem Story

Sinetar, Marsha. *Self-Esteem Is Just an Idea We Have about Ourselves*. New York: Paulist, 1991.

50. The Physical Plane

Klein, Bob. *Movements of Magic: The Spirit of T'ai-Chi-Ch'uan*. North Hollywood, CA: Newcastle, 1984.

Turner, Kristina. *The Self-Healing Cookbook: A Macrobiotic Primer for Healing Body, Mind and Moods with Whole, Natural Food*. Grass Valley, CA: Earthtones, 1987.

51. Initiating Change

Hurston, Zora Neal. *Their Eyes Were Watching God*. New York: HarperCollins, 1990.

52. Ring–Pass–Not

Daly, Mary. *Gyn/Ecology: The Metaethics of Radical Feminism*. Boston: Beacon, 1978. Revised edition, 1990.

Acknowledgments

The idea for this book came to me during a conversation with Emöke B'racz as we sat in a sidewalk cafe one brilliant afternoon in Barcelona. Her enthusiasm for life and canny wisdom inspired me to pursue what I initially thought was a silly idea.

My circle of support during the writing of this book was a wide one, with many people providing inspiration, guidance, money, confidence, and all manner of necessities.

Tom Grady, my editor at HarperSanFrancisco, understood the essential intention of this peculiar book and provided lucid, witty, and consistent encouragement. Leslie Williams, my editor from the Background, informed the manuscript with her incisive political insight and unerring sensitivity to the power of language.

For her inspiring companionship and generosity of spirit, I thank Deborah Brink. For his willingness to discuss everything, anytime, at great length, I thank Red Crowley. For her efficient maintenance of Escapadia Press distribution and consistent friendship, I thank Celeste Tibbets. For his vision, I thank Richard Downing. For their early encouragement, I thank Linda Bryant, Wendy Belkin, Cathy Hope, Jamie Ashe, and the Websters: Celeste Tibbets, Melissa Tidwell, Debra Hiers, and Amanda Gable. For reviewing exercises as they were written and for playing a wicked game of cards, I thank the Shanghai Sisters: Carol Bachman, Rose Dodson, Lynzi Williams, Iris Gersh, Bridget Bernie Tucker, and Ellen Jaffe-Bitz, with a special thanks to Ellen for naming the Nautilus Route. For providing homes for me, I thank Natalie Goldberg, Bridget Bernie Tucker, Molly Moyer, and

Linda Millemann. For their financial, moral, and postcard support, I thank the subscribers to *Fugitive Information*. For a seamless transition and promotional savvy, I thank Lillian Yielding. For easing my way around the world, I thank Michael Granade and Avalon Travel. For their cheerful efficiency and dedication to publishing, I thank Jo Beaton, Kevin Bentley, Clayton Carlson, Ani Chamichian, Terri Goff, Matthew Lore, Pat Rose, Robin Seaman, and the entire staff of HarperSanFrancisco.

To Heart Sisters far and wide, for providing models and inspiration and friendship, I am grateful: Mary Jane Hagan, Dill O'Hagan, Kay Adams, Suzanne Bellamy, Carolyn Bemis, Rebecca Clark, Laura Davis, Joanne DeMark, Alix Dobkin, Linda Finnell, Darcy Greder, Cindy Green-Fisher, Diana Grove, Carol Harrison, Judith Harriss, Marlene Johnson, Cathy McHenry, Denise Messina, Maria Elena Orona, Carol Plummer, Nell Stone, Rita Wuebbeler to name just a few.

Finally, I am grateful to my library of books and all their authors, the beauty of northern New Mexico, my courage to speak, and the moon.